AMERICAN COUNTRY LIVING

STENCILS

TECHNIQUES, PATTERNS, AND MORE

AMERICAN COUNTRY LIVING

STENCILS

TECHNIQUES, PATTERNS, AND MORE

TIMOTHY W. FREW

STENCIL DESIGNS BY RICHARD KOLLATH, DRAWN BY LISA WEINER

ARCH CAPE PRESS

New York

This 1991 edition published by Arch Cape Press,
distributed by Outlet Book Company, Inc.,
a Random House Company,
225 Park Avenue South,
New York, New York 10003.

ISBN 0-517-02016-5

AMERICAN COUNTRY LIVING: STENCILS
was prepared and produced by
Michael Friedman Publishing Group, Inc.
15 West 26th Street
New York, New York 10010

Editor: Sharon Kalman
Art Director: Jeff Batzli
Layout: Helayne Messing
Photography Researcher: Daniella Jo Nilva

Typeset by Bookworks Plus
Color separation by Scantrans Pte. Ltd.
Printed and bound in Hong Kong by Leefung-Asco Printers, Ltd.

8 7 6 5 4 3 2 1

DEDICATION

To my grandmother, Virginia Ulrich, for all the hours in the garden and the many conversations over lunch. I will remember them always.

ACKNOWLEDGMENTS

I would like to thank Richard Kollath, whose name is synonymous with "Arts and Crafts." Working with him has always been a pleasure. I would also like to thank Sharon Kalman, my editor on this and several other projects. She's always been a good friend and a patient editor, despite the numerous deadlines I've missed.

CONTENTS

INTRODUCTION

There is an immediate and rewarding satisfaction in working with stencils. The process is easy, and the results appear right before your eyes. A procedure that has historic roots, the art of stenciling has not changed drastically from that of centuries ago. It is a printing process for producing an image over and over again. It is a skill that greatly depends on the control and dexterity of the stenciler, but also one that can easily be learned.

Stenciling began as an affordable alternative to wallpaper, rugs, and printed fabrics. Such luxuries weren't widely available or affordable to the average rural homeowner. And, even for those who could afford them, most manufacturers didn't have distributors in the countryside, where most people still lived. Until the Industrial Revolution, wallpaper, rugs, and fabrics were printed and woven by hand, and even after the advent of mechanization, these were luxuries only the gentry could afford. As a result, many people brightened their homes by stenciling colored patterns and designs on walls, floors, furniture, bedclothes, window coverings, and any other surface that seemed appropriate.

In addition to floors and walls, stencils were used for decorating furniture, picture and mirror frames, wood and tin boxes, chests, cupboards, tablecloths, draperies, and more. Stencilers took their inspiration from the things around them. Patterns were taken from china, wallpaper, and fabric designs popular at the time, as well as objects seen in everyday rural life—flowers, fruits, leaves, trees, birds, and barnyard animals.

Usually associated with the early settlers of North America, the art of stenciling has deep traditions and roots in virtually every country of the world. In 2000 B.C., the Egyptians used stencils to decorate the vaults of their dead. Even before that the Chinese used stencils to produce repeated designs on everything from pottery to clothing. It is believed that the earliest stencils were made from animal

© Jessie Walker

Many of today's most popular stencil designs are based on the same simple geometric, floral, and animal motifs that were popular during the colonial era in North America.

hides and papyrus leaves. At the beginning of the second century A.D., the Chinese invented paper, and it wasn't too long before paper stencils began to be used as an early form of printing for religious texts and manuscripts.

With the opening of trade routes between China and the rest of the world, the art of stenciling quickly spread. Japan and India created lovely stenciled fabrics inspired by nature and simple geometric designs.

In Europe, the French and the Italians were the first to delve into the art of stenciling. In fact, the word stencil originates from the old French word *estenceler* ("to sparkle") and the Latin *scintilla* (a "spark"). In the Middle Ages, the French decorated everything from playing cards and games to textiles and wallpaper with colorful stencils. In England, stenciling was used to decorate the walls and furniture of medieval churches.

Today, the stencil offers a wealth of decorating opportunities for the modern home. From the delicately stenciled mantle of a fireplace to the floral elegance of stenciled table linens; from soft hues and down-home images in a country kitchen to teddy bears in a child's bedroom, there is no end to the versatility of the simple stencil. In the modern world of faux finishes, bold clothing, and do-it-yourself interior design, interest in this ancient art is as strong as ever.

Stenciling has a built-in success rate and has always been a perfect vehicle for a beginning artist. While the basic process of stenciling is relatively simple, spectacular results can be achieved through intricate stencil designs and an effective use of color.

The techniques outlined in this book, and the pre-printed stencils included, will provide you with a wide range of rich design possibilities. They can be used by themselves, in multiple color arrangements, or in combination with other stencils.

If you're not experienced with stenciling, then start small; stencil a welcome plaque for your door; your name or house number on your mailbox; or stencil a few flowers and a heart on a wooden birdhouse. It really doesn't matter how much you do or on what, for it is in the act of actually stenciling that the real pleasure comes. When the project is

finished and you see the results, your satisfaction and sense of achievement will inspire you to try larger and more complicated projects. Once you become comfortable with the medium, you will realize that the possibilities are limited only by your imagination.

This book is designed to inspire as well as instruct. As you leaf through these pages, look at the beautiful designs created by other artisans. Borrow from these ideas and incorporate them into your own designs. Once you have mastered the few basic design skills and application techniques, you will see that a whole new world of decorative ideas is yours for the taking.

CHAPTER ONE

TOOLS AND MATERIALS

T he basic techniques involved in stenciling are simple. It takes very little artistic ability to perform all of the tasks necessary to complete a stencil project. There are, however, a few skills that must be mastered in order to attain the most beautiful results. As with most artistic endeavors, having the proper tools and equipment at hand is half the battle.

Whether you plan on designing and creating your own intricate stencil patterns or just using a few of the designs provided in this book for a simple stencil project, you will still need to purchase a few inexpensive items in order to get started on your new hobby. The following chapter provides a guide to the different tools and materials you will need. Many of these items can be used for other crafts projects besides stenciling. The number and variety of materials you buy will, to a certain extent, depend on how involved you plan on getting in the craft of stenciling. There is one thing to keep in mind, however, when purchasing tools and materials for any craft: Do not skimp on quality. Inadequate brushes, cheap paints, and poor quality materials will lead to nothing but frustration for any would-be artisan.

BRUSHES

A complete set of high-quality brushes is probably the most important component of a stenciler's kit. Never skimp when it comes to buying stencil brushes. Poor quality brushes will lead to nothing but headaches in the long run. The bristles will quickly fall out, and paint will not go on evenly.

A stencil brush is vastly different from an ordinary paint brush. Designed to be held like a pencil, the traditional stencil brush is short and stubby and has stiff hog's hair bristles that are cut flat at the end. Instead of using a stroking motion as in most types of painting, the stenciler holds the brush perpendicular to the surface and applies the paint with a tapping motion. By varying the speed and intensity of this tapping, or pouncing motion, the stenciler can control the depth of color and shading of the design.

Stencil brushes vary in size from ⅕ of an inch to 2 inches (.5 cm to 5 cm). The size of the brush you use depends on the size of the opening on the stencil you are applying—the larger the opening, the larger the brush. It is best to have several different brush sizes on hand so that you are ready for anything. In addition, you should have a separate brush for each different color of paint you are using on your stencil design. This way you will not have to stop and clean your brushes every time you want to switch to a different color. If you do use the same brush for two or more colors, make sure it is thoroughly cleaned and dried to avoid any unwanted mixing of colors. To clean oil-based paints from a brush use either turpentine or mineral spirits. To clean water-based paints, use a mild soap and warm water.

Stencil brushes also come in a variety of different handle lengths and widths. The type of handle you use is largely a matter of personal preference, although short-handled brushes are generally easier to use when stenciling in and around tight areas. Before purchasing your brushes, pick each one up and hold it. Test its balance and how it feels in your hand. If you are a beginner, you may want to try a variety of handle lengths until you find the brush style that best suits your technique. Before using a new brush, twirl its head between your fingers to remove any loose bristles. Wash it thoroughly, using one of the two methods described in the previous paragraph. Make sure it is completely dry before using it.

THE STENCILS

Beginning on page 90 are more than twenty-five different pre-printed stencil motifs. There are designs suitable for children, French country motifs, a beautiful selection of floral and nature-inspired designs, as well as stencils that echo the traditional qualities of Early America. In addition to the main stencil designs, there is a selection of matching stencil borders that can be used in combination with the main stencils, as part of an overall design, or they may just as easily be used separately. Whatever your specific needs, there are myriad creative possibilities within this collection of stencils. To use these designs, cut the pages directly from the book and use them as actual stencil templates, or preferably, transfer them to heavy-duty stencil paper, a stencil card, acetate, or Mylar® by using either tracing paper or a photocopier.

If you do use these pages as stencil templates, or if you transfer them to a stencil card or some other sort of un-coated heavy paper, it will be necessary to treat the paper with a combination of turpentine and linseed oil to help protect the stencils (see page 26).

In addition to using the motifs provided here, I encourage you to design your own stencil patterns. You can find inspiration for these stencil designs all around you. Just keep in mind that you will be dealing only with silhouettes. Look around the room at the objects you have collected and imagine how they would look in silhouette and as a repeated pattern. Also, look at magazines, at printed or woven fabrics, and at china and earthenware. Any of these can provide inspiration for a stencil design.

WHAT TYPE OF STENCIL PAPER SHOULD I USE

The complexity and involvement of your project—whether it is a small box or an entire room—will, for the most part, dictate what type of material you use for your stencil template. For small projects, such as a box, an article of clothing, or even a small piece of furniture, you can use **stencil paper**. This semi-transparent waxed paper is inexpensive and easy to use. Because you can see through it, stencil paper allows you to cut a stencil from a design placed directly beneath it, eliminating the need to transfer a design to the template. The problem with stencil paper is that it is not very durable and, therefore, not good for large projects or repeated uses.

One step up from stencil paper, is **stencil card** or **oaktag**. This is a thick piece of flexible paper that in most cases has been treated with linseed oil to give it a smooth, impermeable surface. Untreated stencil card is also widely available; however, it should be treated with a combination of turpentine and linseed oil before it is used. This is the material that most widely resembles the stencils used in the past. Designs can be drawn or photocopied directly onto it, it is easy to cut, and it is strong enough to handle extremely intricate designs. Stencil card is not transparent, however, so registration marks must be used to line up the templates precisely when applying the stencils. Beginners may find it difficult to work with stencil card because the surface below the stencil cannot be seen.

One of the best materials for making stencils is **acetate**. These thin, transparent plastic sheets come in a variety of sizes and gauges. For most stenciling projects, I recommend using a sheet of acetate between .0075 and .010 gauge. When using strips of acetate to make long straight lines, it is best to use thicker, stronger gauges. Acetate is extremely durable and can withstand repeated uses. In fact, with proper care, acetate stencils should last for years.

Stencil outlines are drawn directly onto the acetate with a technical marking pen filled with permanent ink. Any mistakes, however, must be immediately removed with damp cloth before the ink dries. Acetate stencils are great for applying multicolor designs where a different stencil must be used for each color. Because it is transparent, acetate enables you to easily line up the various colors of a single design. The trickiest thing about these plastic stencils is that they are somewhat difficult to cut. If your razor knife becomes at all dull, or if you are cutting intricate curved shapes, the acetate has a tendency to split. To avoid this, always use a very sharp knife and change the blade frequently.

Mylar® is perhaps the most versatile, durable, and easy to use of all the stencil template materials. Mylar® is a trade name for a frosted plastic film that is very similar to acetate. Its main advantage over acetate is that its slightly frosted surface can be drawn on with a pencil, making it easy to correct mistakes. In addition, Mylar® is less rigid than acetate and does not have as great a tendency to split while it is being cut. Available in virtually all art supply stores, Mylar® comes in a range of grades, .004 or .005 being the best for stenciling.

CUTTING UTENSILS

A craft knife with replaceable blades, such as an X-acto® knife, is the ideal cutting tool for any type of stencil material. A sharp knife is essential to successful stenciling. Using a dull knife will result in ragged cuts and may cause you to slip and damage the stencil. These ragged edges and unwanted cuts will then show up on the stenciled surface. You can avoid wasted hours of work and sloppy results by changing the blade in your knife often. A blade can never be too sharp, so always have plenty on hand. Blades can be purchased at any hardware, hobby, stationery, or art supply store.

In addition to a razor knife, you should have a heavier utility knife and a good pair of strong scissors for cutting and trimming sheets of acetate or stencil card to the proper size. Craft-style hole-punchers, which come in many sizes, are also valuable cutting tools for tapping out neat circles from intricate stencil designs.

PAINT

Virtually every type of paint can and has been used in the art of stenciling. In the old days of professional country stencilers, the artisans mixed natural pigments, such as brick dust or clay, with skim milk to make a usable paint. As a result, the colors used in stenciling were often determined by the materials at hand in a particular region. If the area was rich in brown or yellow clay, then these would be the prevailing colors in most stencil designs. In spite of this, the artisans could achieve at least a limited variety of color by mixing the paints. Working from three or four basic colors, the stencilers of old could work and rework the color combinations until they found something they liked.

Today, premixed paints are available in any color, shade, or hue; however, a good working knowledge of color and paint mixing is essential for best results.

In addition to the many colors of paint available, there are also several types of paint that you will need to consider before you begin your stenciling project. Different types of paint have different characteristics and advantages. Your choice of paint depends on what surface you are stenciling and what type of results you are looking for.

ACRYLIC PAINT

Acrylic paints are probably the most versatile and easy to use of all stenciling mediums. They are inexpensive, fast-drying, and are available in an extremely wide variety of premixed colors. Because they are water soluble, acrylics can be cleaned and thinned using ordinary tap water. Once dry, they form a tough skin that will last for years.

These easy-to-use paints are suitable for most dull surfaces that will not receive a lot of wear and tear. If the surface you are stenciling has a high gloss or will receive a lot of traffic you will be better off using japan or some other oil-based paint. Acrylics, however, will adhere to most surfaces. They are suitable for wood, concrete, plaster—virtually any paintable surface. On fabrics, acrylic paint stays pliable and survives repeated washing.

Acrylic paints work especially well on dull, gloss-free surfaces, such as this raw wood basket.

© William Seitz

JAPAN PAINTS

Most professional stencilers prefer to use japan paints for large projects such as walls, floors, ceilings, and large pieces of furniture. Japan paints dry quickly to a matte finish and, like acrylics, are available in a wide range of colors. These paints, however, are oil-based, making mixing and clean-up a bit more involved than with acrylic paints. Japan paints must be cleaned and thinned using either turpentine or mineral spirits. When using these paints you must be very careful to clean up any mistakes or spills immediately. Japan paints are as permanent as they are fast-drying.

Japan paints are ideal for glossy, nonporous surfaces such as glazed ceramics, metal, glass, and plastics. They are also a bit more durable than acrylics, so if you are stenciling a floor, or some other area that will receive a lot of wear and tear, japan paints may be your best choice.

SPRAY PAINTS

In recent years, many artisans have experimented with the use of spray paints in stenciling. The effect that these enamel paints produce can be very lovely and is somewhat different from the stippled effect created by a brush. Proper use of these paints, however, requires a steady and practiced hand. If the paint is applied too quickly it has a tendency to run under the stencil. The stencils must be firmly in place, and the paint must be applied in short, quick bursts to avoid this problem.

SETTING UP A WORK SPACE

Prior to beginning any creative project it is essential to establish a good work space. This may be a temporary space that you set up before you work and then return to its original use when you finish, or a space that you permanently establish that will only be used for craft projects.

THE SURFACE

No matter where you do your stenciling, begin with ample room and an uncluttered working space. The required elements are few. A firm, steady work surface such as a kitchen table, a work table, or a table you construct out of a heavy surface on solid sawhorses is essential. This work surface can be in the garage, in the basement, or in the kitchen; the location is not as important as the sturdiness of the surface. Stenciling requires consistent pressure and a gentle pouncing of the stencil brush onto the stenciling surface. A card table or any similar light-framed table may wiggle and impede your working rhythm, and the results could be disastrous.

The table should be high enough so that you don't have to bend over too far to do your work. A good guideline is to have a table that is level with, or just above your belly button when you are seated at a chair. Of course, if you work standing up the table should be higher. Nothing takes the fun out of a craft project quicker than a sore back and a stiff neck.

Stenciling projects require a great deal of cutting. To protect your work table lay down one or two layers of cardboard. It is best to tape down the cardboard with masking tape to prevent it from slipping. In the process of cutting away the printed pattern you will be cutting through the stencil paper and into the layer of cardboard underneath. Be sure to change the undersurface when needed to eliminate a build-up of ruts, which may throw the knife blade off course and damage the stencil.

The best surface for cutting stencils is a glass cutting mat. Simply purchase a sheet of ¼-inch (.6 cm) thick glass cut to approximately 12 inches by 12 inches (30 cm by 30 cm). Either have the edges filed down or cover them with masking tape. Also, it is a good idea to paint the underside of the glass white so that if you are using acetate stencils, the outlines will show up. The blade will move along smoothly without creating ruts or gouges. You will also find that this type of cutting board doubles nicely as a palette for mixing paints.

Another cutting surface option is a self-healing cutting mat, which can be purchased at an art supply store. These rubberized mats have a surface that will close up immediately after cutting. The main drawback of self-healing mats is that the knife blade tends to drag more than on a glass cutting mat.

THE LIGHT SOURCE

Ample light is essential to a proper work space. If possible, set up your space near a window. Natural light is always pleasant, and tends not to distort color as much as artificial fluorescent light. It is important, however, to supplement natural light with an incandescent light source. Clip-on lamps provide mobility and are handy for directing light to specific areas. These lamps are inexpensive and readily available at most hardware stores. When situating your lamps, try to prevent casting unwanted shadows on your work area. Experiment by adding or moving lights until the work area is as bright and evenly lit as possible.

It is important to have a sturdy, well-lit table on which to do your stenciling. It is best to take advantage of natural and incandescent light sources as much as possible, since fluorescent light tends to distort color.

© Ralph Bogertmann

THE WATER SOURCE

Because you are working with paint, it is necessary to have a source of water nearby. This can be a sink or a plastic bucket or bowl that you keep within reach. Acrylic paint cleans up so well with tap water and a mild soap that even the kitchen sink is an acceptable source. As long as you carefully rinse all surfaces, you will not damage the sink. If you are working with oil-based paints and turpentine you will want to use a utility sink rather than your kitchen sink for cleanup. Also, you should have an ample supply of paper towels or newsprint on hand to clean up spills and reduce unwanted mess.

HELPFUL TOOLS

Additional materials that will help you with measuring and cutting include: a T-square, a clear plastic triangle (being able to see through your triangle is a great advantage), a tape measure, a plumb line, masking tape, a metal ruler for use as a cutting edge, an S-curve, a palette knife, a sturdy pair of scissors, a sharp pencil, and, as stated earlier, plenty of paper, cardboard, and extra razor blades. Paper of all kinds and sizes seems to always come in handy for masking out an area of the stencil, for testing out a possible design, for sketching out a completely new design, or simply for use as scrap paper. I find drawing paper, tracing paper, and graph paper all essential components of my studio inventory.

MAINTAINING YOUR WORK SPACE

Almost as important as having a comfortable well-lit work space is keeping that work space clean and organized once you begin your work. Keep your materials in order. Always have plenty of rags or paper towels on hand to wipe up any spills. Paints should always be stored tightly covered. Periodically clean your hands to avoid smudging paint on your finished project. It is also very important to avoid a build-up of dried paint on the stencil card. Too much paint build-up will produce a fuzzy and distorted edge.

A gummed-up stencil brush can also lead to mistakes or accidents. Check the brush periodically and clean it with warm water and a mild soap. If you do clean your stencil brush in the middle of a project, be sure to dry it completely so that the excess water does not dilute the quality of the colors. Always do a test blot before going back to the stencil.

By keeping an orderly work space as well as clean hands and tools you will avoid countless mishaps. However, no matter how careful you are, the occasional accident is bound to happen. Don't panic; acrylic paint is easily cleaned from most surfaces with a damp cloth while it is still wet and oil-based paints can be cleaned with a quick application of turpentine or mineral spirits.

CHAPTER TWO

BASIC
TECHNIQUES

O nce your design plan is finalized, it is time to actually begin stenciling. While the entire process is fairly simple, it does require several basic steps that must be carefully followed for optimum success. These include transferring the designs to stencil card, acetate, or Mylar®; cutting out the stencil; measuring the project; preparing the surface; mixing the paint; applying the paint; and, finally, sealing the project.

None of these techniques is extremely difficult, but, all will require a certain amount of practice before they can be mastered. This chapter provides a basic outline for the various techniques involved in this craft. Through practice and repetition you will be able to expand upon these basic techniques and begin creating a working style of your own.

If you are not accustomed to using a razor knife, practice cutting out several working designs. Learn which cutting angles are easiest for you and develop your techniques for cutting out difficult curves and circles. Mixing paints and developing a personalized palette is a challenge that can perplex the most experienced of artists. The more you work with your paints, the more comfortable you will feel with color. If you are new at stenciling start off with a few small, simple projects consisting of only two or three basic colors. After you successfully complete these, you will be more at ease with the stenciling process, and then be able to go on to more involved projects.

TRANSFERRING THE DESIGNS

When transferring a stencil design to stencil board or an acetate or Mylar® sheet be sure to allow a margin of at least one or two inches (2.5 to 5 cm) around the pattern to help keep the stencil strong.

While there are several methods for transferring designs, the simplest is to use a photocopier. Most modern photocopiers are capable of copying onto fairly heavy stencil board and even acetate. In a matter of seconds you can make enough copies of a single motif for a many-colored design.

If you don't have access to a photocopier and are using stencil board or paper, use carbon paper instead. Simply sandwich the carbon paper—carbon side down—between your design and the stencil board and secure it with masking tape. Next, trace around the outline of the design using either a hard pencil or a fine-tipped burnisher. Once the carbon design is transferred to the paper go over it again with a dark, fibre-tipped pen.

Another method is to trace your design onto tracing paper using a soft pencil, leaving as thick a layer of graphite as possible on the paper. Then place the tracing paper—graphite side down—on top of the stencil paper and secure with masking tape. Trace over the outline again using a hard pencil. The process should leave an outline on the stencil paper. Darken the outline with a fibre-tipped pen.

If you are using acetate or Mylar®, simply lay the sheet directly over the top of the stencil design, secure it with masking tape, and transfer the motif by using a technical drawing pen. Note: Water-based inks, such as in most fibre-tipped pens, will not hold on acetate. You must use permanent ink on acetate.

CUTTING THE STENCIL

The most important thing to remember when cutting out your stencils is to make sure you know what gets cut out and what remains on the stencil. This sounds simple, but be careful; your eyes can play tricks on you, and, before you know it, you've made an incorrect cut. Do not cut the small bridges that separate one part of the design from another, as they hold the entire design together. If you do cut one of these bridges, carefully repair it with a small piece of masking tape.

The most successful way to cut stencils is to always use a sharp blade, a smooth undersurface, and even pressure that allows the knife blade to glide smoothly along the printed pattern. Again, remember to always have extra blades for your razor knife on hand; when the blade feels dull, put in a new one. A sharp blade is half the cutting battle so don't be stingy.

The most efficient way to cut a stencil is to maintain a downward cutting motion, rotating the stencil as need be. Use a light, constant pressure and try to lift the blade as little as possible. A few long cuts are much smoother than a lot of short cuts. A straight-edge ruler or an S-curve can be a great help when confronting long lines in a design. Many stencilers recommend securely taping the stencil down to the cutting surface before making a cut. This will prevent the stencil from slipping during the cutting process. I find, however, that keeping the stencil mobile makes cutting much easier. This way, you can turn and shift the stencil to achieve the best cutting angle possible. The best of both worlds can be achieved by using a glass cutting mat. Then you can secure the stencil to the cutting surface and still have the freedom to rotate stencil and cutting mat together.

The stencils included in this book are printed on thin paper. As stated earlier, I recommend transferring the designs to stencil card or acetate to provide sturdier stencils. If you choose to use the actual pages as your stencil, or if you transfer the designs to uncoated paper, you must treat these stencils with a protectant prior to use. This will aid in cleaning the templates as well as prevent them from soaking up too much excess paint. A thin coat of wax, acrylic spray, or linseed oil works well in protecting the stencil for repeated use. When using thick stencil card, rub a thin layer of turpentine on the stencil before treating it with linseed oil. This will help compress the paper and make it easier to cut.

© Christopher C. Bain

MEASURING A PROJECT

SINGLE MOTIF

If you are stenciling a single shape onto an object, first find the center of the surface that is going to be stenciled. Even if you don't want the stencil perfectly centered, this will give a good reference point from which you can make adjustments if necessary. Make short vertical and horizontal lines across the surface, forming a cross or plus mark at its center. Then, using this mark as a reference point, hold the stencil in various places until you have found the position you want and mark it with a light pencil line. When you decide on the best placement, fasten the stencil down with masking tape.

Another method of finding the correct positioning for the stencil is to make a cut-out copy or actual proof of your stencil motif and use it as a template for finding a position. When it looks right, replace the proof with the real stencil and begin the process.

REGISTER MARKS

Register marks are used for lining up a stencil if you intend to duplicate the design horizontally, vertically, or diagonally, or if you want to make multiple color stencils (see below). They determine the location or placement of the cut stencil design in relation to the overall surface. They ensure the proper alignment and even spacing of the stencil by remaining a fixed constant. If you use a border pattern, the register marks will allow you to keep the spacing of the repeated image even, while eliminating a great deal of measuring.

MULTIPLE MOTIFS AND BORDERS

Stencil borders and multiple motifs can be placed in various ways on any surface. The trick is to keep these repeating patterns running straight and spaced evenly. This is where register marks come in handy (see above). The use of a cardboard template will also help. For example, let's assume you want to stencil a simple border running along the top of a wall. The first step is to determine exactly how far from the ceiling the border should be. Eyeball it, measure it, adjust and readjust it until you have the perfect distance. Then measure a piece of cardboard to use as a template to fit between the stencil and the ceiling. The dimension of the template should be adjusted to the border you have chosen. Fit the top edge of the template against the ceiling, and the bottom edge against the top of the stencil. This will place the border at a consistent distance from the ceiling. Tape down the stencil and apply the paint. Then move the stencil over and line it up using the template and register marks. Simply repeat this process across the room, being sure to carefully line up and tape down the stencil before applying any paint. When you apply tape to your original stencil always be very careful that you don't rip the bridges.

Another method for stenciling a border is simply to measure the distance you want the border to be from the ceiling, and draw a line the length of the wall, being very careful that it is as straight as possible. Then use that line as a guide for the register marks on the stencil.

Single motifs can often be measured by eye. If, however, the project calls for a series of repeated motifs, such as with this wall border, careful measuring and planning will be necessary.

If you are working out a placement for a large focal design in the center of a wall with a border leading up to it, you must start from the main design and work out from it. Mark a guide line along the length of the wall as described above. Then mark where you want the main design to fall. If the actual design is too large or too small, you can adjust it with a photocopier (see page 26). Then tape down the main design and apply it first. Next apply the border, working out from the main design.

To stencil a vertical border, use a plum line to mark a straight vertical guide line. Then check this guide line with the architectural line of the wall by using a right angle. Not all walls and ceilings are architecturally pure, especially in older houses. You may have to do some adjusting in order to get a usable guide line.

Ultimately, what is most important is the visual balance on the surface. Scale and proportion are the key elements in making the overall design work. Rely on your eye, and ask others to look at it before applying any paint. It is better to take the extra time to carefully lay out a project than to apply paint hastily and regret it later on.

The technique for stenciling borders is explained in greater detail in Chapter Four.

PREPARING THE SURFACE

What kinds of surfaces can you stencil on? Well, just about anything. The best and most receptive surfaces are smooth ones, but you may apply a stencil on barn siding or cement, it is entirely up to you. Again, acrylic paints work well on most surfaces, except for high-gloss finishes, glass, and shiny metals. In these cases, japan paints are a better choice. Always read the information on the tube or can before using any type of paint. Some surface preparation is always necessary before the stenciling process can begin.

Courtesy Stencil-Ease

PAINTED WALLS AND
WAXED OR TREATED WOOD

Wash painted walls with mild soap and warm water and clean wood of any wax build up. Using a little #0 or #00 gauge steel wool on the surface will give the paint a greater holding quality. Try to avoid stenciling raw wood, at least at first, since it will absorb your paint into the untreated fibers, making it very difficult to hide any mistakes. It is best to treat the raw wood with a thin coat of sealer before stenciling on it.

PAPER

Most papers will provide you with a base for stenciling. However, smooth papers work better than coarse ones, since the paint will not bleed as easily. You can create your own birthday or holiday cards as well as develop pictures you might later frame. You might want to try stenciling signs for school or community work.

FABRIC

There is a multitude of possibilities when stenciling on fabric. You can decorate T-shirts or sweat shirts, ornament sheets, or adorn table cloths and napkins with beautiful patterns. Your home is an endless source of possibilities. Try stenciling some curtains or pillows for your porch. Use a stencil design along with a printed fabric or a checked pattern to create your own unique patterns. Fabrics are a versatile foundation for building creative projects.

Acrylic paint takes well to fabric and is machine washable, but you may also wish to explore some of the specific fabric paints available. Be sure to follow the directions on the paint container before mixing fabric paints, then follow the general printing instructions in this book. The technique is always the same.

Stenciling fabric is easy; however, there are a few rules you should follow to achieve the best results. If you intend to wash the fabric often, wash and iron it before applying the stencil. This will remove the sizing from the cloth and make it more receptive to the paint. If you are preparing fabric for drapes, you may work directly on the unwashed material.

Natural fibers take fabric paints better, but acrylic and textile paints will work well on all materials and fibers. Again, if you use specific fabric paint always follow the printed information provided on the package.

Fabric is porous and paint will penetrate through the fibers onto the undersurface. Change the undersurface often to avoid making a mess. When printing on fabric, it is usually better to use a cloth undersurface. Also, be sure the undersurface is directly under the layer of cloth you are stenciling. For example, if you are stenciling a T-shirt, put a piece of cloth inside the T-shirt to prevent the paint from bleeding through to the back of the fabric. Mistakes cannot be removed from fabric. Take the fabric off of the undersurface once you have stenciled it so that it doesn't stick to it. Placing a piece of cardboard under a garment will help it to hold its shape and prevent the paint from seeping through the garment.

When working with fabrics, the work table should be covered with cloth. I usually secure a soft but firm underpadding to the work table with duct tape. This provides a solid bed to stencil on and allows the necessary "give" for the pouncing of the stencil brush.

OTHER SURFACES

Baskets, tables, chests, porch furniture, and other wood projects are all good materials for stencil designs. As your skill develops, larger and more complicated projects will be possible. Again, always check the surface you intend to stencil. If it seems very smooth, rub it with a little steel wool or some very fine sandpaper.

Virtually any hue, tint, or tone can be achieved through the careful mixing of paints. A good working knowledge of color is extremely helpful in planning and executing a stenciling project.

Courtesy Hudson River Museum

MIXING THE PAINTS

No matter how complex, well-planned, or beautifully conceived a stencil project is, its success or failure is ultimately determined by the use of color. The degree of refinement and complexity you wish to give your finished stencil project depends on how well you choose and mix your colors.

Art supply stores offer a wide selection of premixed colors. Depending on how involved you wish the project to

be, it may not be necessary to mix your own colors. Your options, however, can be further enhanced by mixing paints to achieve a nearly endless array of hues, tints, and tones. I suggest purchasing up to twelve different premixed colors. This will provide you with a good base from which to work. Here is a selection of paints which can be used as is or mixed to attain virtually any color needed: magenta, lavender, royal blue, green, both light and dark brown, orange, red, gold, yellow, white, and black.

© Robert Perron/Stencil design by Leslie Power

Always use a separate dish for each color. Open the jar of paint and take out a small amount with a palette knife or an old kitchen knife and immediately return the lid to the jar. If you are mixing paints, use the palette knife to thoroughly blend the colors together until there is no trace of either original color left. Do not use the stencil brush for mixing paints. It is important to keep that brush as clean as possible.

Be sure to mix enough paint for your project, but remember that both acrylic and japan paints dry rapidly. If you notice your paints drying out as you are working, add a small drop of water to acrylic paint or mineral spirits to japan paint to keep the pigment workable.

Once you have arrived at the palette of colors you like, practice stenciling on some scrap paper that has a similar background color to the object you are intending to stencil. This testing process helps prevent mistakes and is well worth your time. Make adjustments to your color until you have found just what you are looking for. Once you have the paint on the walls it will be too late to make drastic color changes.

Always have plenty of water or mineral spirits on hand when working with paint. An old jar or a coffee can works well for this purpose. The water or mineral spirits will come in handy for thinning paint, correcting mistakes, and for cleaning the stencil brush. Never leave a paint-covered stencil brush sitting for very long. If it dries, you will have a pretty, but useless, brush. Mild soap and water will clean the brush easily if the acrylic is still wet, and turpentine or mineral spirits will do the job on japan paint. If you are leaving your work for a few hours and don't want to go through the trouble of thoroughly cleaning your brushes, wrap them securely in aluminum foil to keep them from drying out.

APPLYING THE PAINT

Once the stencil has been secured to the surface with masking tape, take the stencil brush in hand and lightly dab the brush into the paint a few times until only the tip of the brush is thoroughly coated. Then blot the brush on some paper towels to remove the excess paint, being sure to leave enough for the painting process. Getting the proper amount of paint on your brush is a simple process that is critical to success; it does take some practice.

Using short, stabbing strokes, dab the color into the cut areas of the stencil. Only work with one color at a time. In most cases you should cut out a separate stencil for each color. However, if the area you are coloring is small, you may simply block out the part of the stencil design that does not receive that particular color. Use waxed paper, typing paper, or additional pieces of stencil paper to cover the areas you do not wish the paint to go through. A small piece of masking tape will work equally well. (Take care not to lift off the small bridges.) Blocking out these areas provides greater freedom.

The density or fullness of a particular color depends on the degree of pressure you apply when dabbing. Color saturation is determined through mixing, but if you apply the pigment lightly, the image or painted shape will appear faint. The tricky balance is to know how much paint to leave on the stencil brush and how much pressure to apply when dabbing. Practice is the best teacher. You may consider testing your technique on a surface similar to the one you intend to use for your final surface. Newsprint is also a good testing ground for working out technical control and color combinations. This will give you a chance to master the process before actually beginning. It is also possible to add shading or vary the tone of a specific area of the design by shifting the pressure on the brush. The more you experiment, the greater your control over the medium.

Allow yourself the time and flexibility to play with the materials. This book provides you with a great potential for understanding the foundations and techniques of the art of stenciling.

Use a smooth, constant stroke when cutting out the stencil design. The fewer times you lift the razor knife of the stencil, the fewer jagged edges you will have. If you do get ragged edges, use a piece of fine sandpaper to smooth them down. A straight edge and an S-curve are extremely helpful tools when cutting out a stencil.

Once the stencil is cut out, tape it securely to the surface you wish to paint. Adjust, readjust, measure, and eyeball it until you have the exact position you want.

Put a small amount of paint on a plate or palette and lightly dab the end of the stencil brush into it, being careful to only cover the tip of the brush with paint. Remove excess paint from the brush by dabbing it on a paper towel.

Apply the paint to the open areas of the stencil using a light pouncing motion. Never use a stroking motion. The pouncing motion will apply a smooth, even layer of paint.

Add more paint to the brush as needed, making sure not to saturate the bristles. An overloaded brush will cause the paint to run. When applying more than one color to a stencil, complete one entire color before moving on to the next.

Once the stencil is applied, carefully lift the template off of the surface, being careful not to smudge the paint.

© Ralph Bogertmann

PROTECTING THE PROJECT

Even though acrylic and oil-based japan paints are very durable, it may be necessary to protect your project with a sealant. This will depend on how much wear and tear the painted stencils will receive. How you seal your project largely depends on the type of surface you are stenciling. Fabrics stenciled with acrylics or fabric paints need only be sealed with a hot iron and then gently washed. In most cases, wall stencils do not need to be sealed at all, unless they are lower down on the wall and in an area that receives a lot of traffic, such as a hallway.

Most projects, however, require some sort of protection so that the paints will last through the years. Polyurethane varnish is the most commonly used sealant available today. It is easy to use and provides a durable water-resistant film on any painted surface. Polyurethane is available in gloss, semigloss, and matte finishes. Gloss produces a clear, highly lacquered look; semigloss gives a naturally polished silky sheen; and matte has no shine at all.

Before applying any varnish to your project, make sure the stencil paints are completely dry. For oil-based paint wait at least twenty-four hours. Acrylic paints dry much faster, but you should wait for at least six hours before applying varnish. Apply two or three coats of varnish to the project, making sure that each coat is completely dry before applying the next. For large projects, apply the varnish with a flat, one- to two-inch (2.5-to 5-cm) paintbrush, being careful to avoid brush marks. Spray varnish is great for small projects. Follow the instructions on the can.

There is the possibility that the varnish you use will cause the paint to bleed slightly. This is especially true with red pigments. Always read the labels of both the varnish and the paint cans to be sure you are using the correct combinations. In addition, test a small area of the stencil before applying varnish to the whole project.

Once your project is sealed it should last for years under normal wear and tear. At times it may be necessary to touch up both the paint and the varnish. There is more information on protecting your projects in the chapters that follow.

SMALL OBJECTS

The stencil is the perfect medium for decorating a wide array of small objects, from toys, wooden boxes, and picture frames to wrapping paper, stationery, greeting cards, and placemats. Virtually everything that can be painted can be stenciled. Objects with smooth surfaces will take a stencil much better than those with uneven surfaces.

While many people think of stenciling chiefly as a means for embellishing walls, floors, or furniture, artisans throughout history have been using the medium as an inexpensive way to put personal decorative touches on otherwise mundane items. In fact, if you are a novice stenciler I strongly recommend that you direct your first endeavor toward a small object, such as a Shaker box, a picture frame, or a greeting card. This will give you an opportunity to become comfortable with the medium and the basic elements of design and color before you tackle a larger, more permanent project. The basic concepts of design, placement, measurement, and application are essentially the same for smaller objects; however, because you will be working within a limited space with fewer variables, it will be much easier to achieve success.

Look around you. Practically every object you see could be enhanced by the addition of a well-placed stencil. A wastepaper basket, a tissue box, a bread basket, a planter—all of these objects offer possibilities to the creative stenciler. An old cookie sheet can be transformed into a colorful serving tray; a hat box can be turned into a lovely container for cosmetics, letters, or bric-a-brac; even an old mayonnaise jar can be transformed into a bank for a child with the application of a few stencils.

DESIGNING SMALL-SCALE STENCILS

If there is one thing to keep in mind when developing a stencil design for a small object, it is not to get too carried away with it and over-stencil the object. Because you will be working within a tight, confined area, a little bit of stenciling goes a long way. If you let loose with your brush, stencils, and paint, the result will look jumbled at best. Subtlety is a wonderful aspect of any stenciling project, large or small. When working with a box or a picture frame, it is easy to get carried away in the process. A bit of refined, intricate stenciling can be much more effective than an overwhelming mishmash of flowers, borders, and cross-hatching.

The use of a stencil key can be very helpful when designing a pattern or a series of motifs for a small object. This entails making a template, or a tracing, of the various surfaces of the object you will be stenciling (a box or a jar, for instance). By converting your three-dimensional object into several two-dimensional surfaces, you will be able to get a good overall idea of how the pattern will ultimately fit on each surface.

First, trace each of the surfaces of the object onto a separate piece of tracing paper. Next, tape each of the templates you have just made to a separate piece of graph paper, lining it up with the grid on the paper. This will help you to center your design, as well as to line up and space each of the motifs.

Sketch the main motifs you will be using in your project on separate pieces of graph paper, making several copies if you will be using repeated motifs (this is where a photocopier comes in handy), and cut each of them out. Now you have a graph paper record of each surface, as well as loose motif templates that you can rearrange to come up with your design. As you move the various elements around try to achieve a balance and spacing that is pleasing to the eye and appropriate for the size of the surface you are working with. As you develop your design, you may realize that the

motifs you are using are either too large or too small. Once again, a photocopier is great for making fine adjustments in size. If you don't have that luxury, make sketches by hand, using graph paper as a reference.

When you are happy with the design, carefully attach each element to the template with rubber cement or transparent tape. Next, either photocopy the final design onto a piece of stencil paper or carefully trace it onto tracing paper and transfer it to stenciling paper using one of the methods outlined in Chapter Two. Once you have repeated this process for each of the surfaces of your project, you will have a complete set of premeasured stencils ready to cut and apply.

Courtesy Adele Bishop

TINWARE

Painted tinware, or toleware, was once a staple of the colonial household. Brightly colored pitchers, cups, candlesticks, trays, coffeepots, and other tin pieces were sold by "tinmen" who traveled from town to town. These light, decorative items offered an inexpensive way for colonial families to brighten up their otherwise rather drab interiors.

The tinware was both hand-painted and stenciled, usually on a thickly lacquered or painted surface. The colorful designs consisted of motifs taken directly from rural life. Intricate borders would frame lavish decorations of fruits, flowers, animals, even highly detailed barnyard scenes.

The favorite objects for this type of tinware decoration were serving trays, which came in a wide range of sizes and shapes; hinged document boxes, the colonial version of the safety deposit box; buckets, used primarily as planters or spittoons; and coffeepots and pitchers.

With today's growing interest in the rural lifestyle of eighteenth century colonial America, decorative tinware is again becoming popular. Craft stores, flea markets, and county fairs often offer an array of stenciled and hand-painted tinware. It is much more satisfying, however, to purchase plain tinware from the hardware store and decorate it yourself using stencils. Tin watering cans, buckets, pitchers, mugs, trays, and boxes can all be transformed into beautiful decorative items.

The process for decorating a piece of tinware in the traditional way is simple; however, there are several steps you must follow for optimum results. If you are stenciling a piece of old tinware with traces of paint or varnish on it, first remove all of the paint with a commercial paint stripper. Next, use a coarse piece of steel wool to smooth the surface of the tin. The smoother you get the surface, the better your final results will be. If the metal is rusted or pitted, go over it with rust remover and sand it smooth with a fine sandpaper, then wash the piece thoroughly with soap and water and wipe it clean with a tack cloth to remove any stubborn dirt.

Next, apply two coats of metal primer to prevent the tin from rusting in the future as well as to give the background paint a good surface on which to adhere. Allow at least twenty-four hours for the primer to dry after each coat. After the final coat is completely dry, rub it down with a piece of fine steel wool to roughen the surface a bit for the background paint and to eliminate any brush marks. Then use a tack cloth to remove any dust from the surface.

Now apply at least two coats of background paint to the tinware. Use a flat, oil-based paint in any color you choose. The traditional tinware artists primarily use black, red, or yellow for the background. The color you use will largely depend on the colors you have chosen for the stencil design. Again, allow the paint to dry thoroughly between coats and gently rub the surface with steel wool before you begin stenciling.

The most difficult aspect to stenciling tin is getting the paint to the proper consistency because the metal is very hard and smooth. It is best to use japan paints on this type of surface. Water-based paints have a difficult time adhering to tin. When stenciling on tin, it is best to pay less attention to shading and more to producing sharp outlines.

After the stenciling is complete, allow it to dry for about three days and apply a coat or two of varnish to protect the final work. Many artisans also like to give the tinware a final coat of clear paste wax for a soft sheen.

BORDERS

The border is the most traditional of all stencil forms. Throughout the history of the art form, this simple framing device has been an integral part of more elaborate stenciling projects. Walls are rarely stenciled without some sort of border treatment to the frieze, floorboard, chair rail, or all three. Similarly, floors are frequently marked off with some sort of border, either elaborate or simple, before the main stencil design is completed in the middle. Floor borders are also used to highlight rugs, tile work, or the plain wood.

The versatility of the stenciled border and its ability to improve proportions, delineate boundaries, compliment ornamentation, and highlight architectural details have made it an extremely effective tool in interior design. Aside from its role within more elaborate projects, the border can be used as a distinct form of decoration on its own. Essentially nothing more than a series of repeated motifs spread out in a straight line, the border is used in every type of traditional stenciling project. Walls, windows, door frames, floors, staircases, floors, floorcloths, furniture, boxes, shelves, curtains, bedspreads, virtually everything that is stenciled receives some sort of border treatment.

The border is a great device for visually altering and improving the proportions of a room. You can compensate for a ceiling which is too high by placing a narrow border at picture-rail height. Such a border will break up the large expanse of space between the floor and ceiling and focus the eye lower on the wall. Another well-placed border at chair-rail height will further serve to alter the visual dimensions of a room. If, on the other hand, you wish to visually increase the height of the ceiling, use borders to form vertical panels on the walls. This will carry the eye upward and make the ceiling appear higher. Take care, however,

not to create too much of a separation of wall areas with borders. This can create a jumbled and confused effect that will overpower the eye. A heightening effect can also be achieved by adding a border either directly above or in place of the baseboard, thereby adding visual weight to the lower part of the room.

The stenciled border has the subtle ability to pull together several aspects of an overall interior design. It can pick up a few elements of a pattern from a curtain, a piece of furniture, or even a set of china that is on display and then integrate it into the design scheme of the room. Use borders to accentuate doorways or archways. Enhance a sloping ceiling by adding a border along the wall just below ceiling height. Run a border around a window and then repeat the design on the bottom edge of the window shade.

Staircases offer a wealth of opportunity for border treatments. Run a thin border just above or below the banister or the baseboard on either side of the stairwell. A vine border running down the stairs themselves can also be quite effective. Add a floral border across each of the stair risers.

The border is most effective when it is not obtrusive; when it compliments a design rather than dominates it. This does not mean that a border has to be uncomplicated. Many of the most effective border designs are quite elaborate, requiring hours of careful planning and artistry. In general, however, executing a stenciled border is a fairly simple process that often looks much more complex than it actually is.

Borders can also be used to give a flat surface a three-dimensional effect. This *trompe l'oeil*, or "trick of the eye" effect has been employed by stencilers for years. By using foreshortening techniques, the stenciler can simulate a plaster relief frieze between a picture rail and the ceiling. Similar relief and three-dimensional effects can be stenciled onto furniture to imitate moldings and carvings.

Courtesy Stencil-Ease

CHOOSING A PATTERN

The first step in creating a border is determining the pattern or motif you wish to use. Ideas for border patterns can come from a number of sources. Usually a border pattern is a much simpler motif than those used in large scale stencil designs. Look around the room you wish to stencil. What motif possibilities does it contain? Look at the carved wood borders on furniture and door frames. Architectural pediments and friezes may offer ideas for border outlines that can help to integrate the whole room. Other great ideas can be found in old tiles, plates, cups, ceramics, quilts, and draperies. You may also find inspiration from art and design movements of the past. Art deco, art nouveau, Victorian, early Egyptian and Greek art, Chinese etchings and prints, or French country motifs may offer the perfect design element for your stenciled border. The stencil designs in the back of this book contain motifs that will suit any taste or decor, from country to geometric to modern.

TECHNIQUES FOR APPLYING BORDERS

The border is a simple device to stencil. The basic techniques for applying these stencils were touched upon in Chapter Two. Depending on how involved and complicated the stencil design is, the exact methods of application may vary. There are several techniques that are specific to borders alone.

Essentially there are two types of borders: those that run in a continuous straight line with a simple repeat, and those that have a larger, more complicated repeat. If the repeat is small and essentially continuous, such as a dentil border, geometric border, or a simple vine, very little measuring and preplanning is needed. You can simply start at one end of the wall and continue on until you reach the other end.

If, however, the border contains larger, more spread out repeating motifs, a little more planning is necessary. You must determine how many times the element will repeat in the given space, and exactly where each element will fall.

© Richard S. Mandelkorn

Ideally you will want the repeating pattern situated in such a way that it avoids ending the border in a partial pattern. Also, you must consider the size of the motif and create a spacing that fits within the proportions of the design. The amount of space between repeats and the final size of the motifs will determine the final effect of the border design. If the stencil pattern will not fit into the space an equal number of times, and if a partial pattern at the end of the border will look awkward, then the size of the pattern may be too large or small for the room or the object you are stenciling. Do a few test proofs of your border on strips of paper. By holding or taping this paper to the wall you can get a pretty good idea of how the final border design will appear and exactly where each element will fall.

MARKING YOUR BORDER

Once you have determined the sizing and spacing of your border design you must carefully mark it out on the surface. Lightly draw a line across the wall where the center of each stencil will line up. Use a soft lead pencil and straight edge to make sure the line is level. If the border is to go around a wall, measure down from the ceiling or up from the floor and mark it off every ten inches (25 cm) or so. If the border is running up the wall, measure from the corner where the two walls meet, or use a plumb bob and chalk box to achieve a straight line. Next, connect the dots with your straight edge. When marking off your project, you may find that the walls, ceilings, and floors of the room are not completely straight. This is especially true in old houses and apartments. As a result your line may curve in places. It is best to straighten out this line as much as possible. If your final border curves along with the wall or ceiling you will end up with an awkward, inaccurate stencil design.

TURNING CORNERS

There are two basic methods for making a right angle (from horizontal to vertical or vice versa) with a stenciled border. The first and simplest way is by "blocking." In this method you stencil out to the end of the horizontal border and then turn the stencil at a right angle and pick up the vertical section flush with the end of the last section you stenciled, basically forming the letter "L" with your border. Mask the end of the first border to prevent any overlapping and buildup of paint on the corner.

The second method, known as "mitering," is a bit more complicated; however, the final results are well worth the extra effort. This method provides a gentle, continuous joint. To achieve a mitered corner, draw a diagonal line at a forty-five degree angle from the corner where the two sides of the border will meet. Place a piece of masking tape or some other type of mask along the line on the opposite side from which you are stenciling. Then, stencil up to and

over the masking tape. Once that section has dried, move the masking tape to the other side of the line to mask the area you just stenciled. Now, continue to stencil in the other direction so that the two sides of the pattern meet at an angle.

If the border design is made up of free-form florals or small, simple geometric patterns, then no real planning is needed at the corners. The design will be easy to pick up when going in another direction. Turn the stencil plate around the corner and pick up the pattern halfway through.

APPLYING A STRIPE

A plain stripe or band is perhaps the simplest type of border to apply. It is also one of the most common borders. Stripes are frequently used around a floor, a piece of furniture, or along a wall. Quite often they are used in conjunction with a more elaborate stencil design; however, they can also be effectively used on their own. As with a more elaborate stenciled border, it is important to carefully mark off the stripe with two parallel lines. It is important that the line is straight and that any curvature of the wall surface is compensated for. For making a striped border, all you need is two long pieces of acetate or stencil board. It is best to use a precut edge rather than an edge you cut yourself, which will not be as straight. Tape one of the sheets of acetate or stencil board to the surface so that the precut edge lines up with one of the lines. Then tape the other piece along the other line. Block each end of the stripe with a piece of masking tape. Apply the paint and move both pieces of acetate down to the next section of the striped border and continue until the stripe is complete.

Turning a corner with a stripe is simple. Stencil up to one edge and then turn at a right angle. Be sure to mask the end of the stripes you have already stenciled to avoid an unwanted buildup of paint.

© Phillip Ennis

CHAPTER FIVE

FLOORS AND FLOORCLOTHS

Just as the American colonialists used stencils as the chief means for decorating their drab walls, they also used stencils to provide colorful and inexpensive decoration for their floors. At the time, carpets and rugs were scarce and expensive so people used paint to adorn their plain wooden floors. The very first stencil and hand-painted floor designs in colonial America were primitive imitations of the rug patterns that were popular in Europe and in the growing cities of Philadelphia and Boston. These designs consisted mostly of simple geometric shapes—a central pattern of checks or diamonds surrounded by a plain striped border.

Today, stenciled floor designs have become more and more elaborate. Some designers lay out intricate floral or woodland scenes—all done with stencils—on their bleached oak floors. Three-dimensional checkerboard patterns and meandering basketweave or grapevine borders are all quite common. Yet, even though modern stenciling techniques and the continual interest in stenciling design have enabled artisans to stretch the boundaries of the medium, more and more people are opting for the simple stenciled floor designs of America's colonial past. Whereas thirty years ago, wall-to-wall shag carpeting was all the rage, today people are tearing up that carpeting to uncover beautiful bare wood floors that hold myriad possibilities for subtle design treatments and schemes.

There are three basic approaches to the stencil design of a wood floor. First, the floor can work as the dominant element in the overall interior design scheme. It can be a colorfully ornate design that serves as the focal point of the

rest of the design scheme. This is usually only possible if you are starting the entire interior design of the room from scratch. It is often difficult to create a dominant presence in a room containing already established elements.

The second approach is to equally balance the impact of the floor design with the other dominant elements of the room. This can be accomplished by picking up a motif from the walls or the fabrics (i.e. draperies, upholstered furniture, etc.) in the room and incorporating them into the design of the floor stencils. You can also use the stencil as a unifying device by bringing together colors or motifs from two seemingly disparate elements already present in the room.

The third approach is to create a minimal effect with the stenciled floor, putting the design emphasis on the walls, furniture, or draperies in the room. Use a delicate pattern on the floor and perhaps just two shades of the same color. A subtle, yet beautiful effect can be achieved by outlining the floor with a simple border pattern and leaving an open expanse of finished wood in the center of the floor. Or, use a border to outline a plain area rug in the center of the room.

Floor stencils provide a very economical and easy way to put a final personalized touch to any interior design scheme. Floor stencils are especially well suited to rooms which receive a lot of wear and tear such as a kitchen, hallway, or child's room. Stenciling is a lot cheaper than carpeting and, if properly applied, will last much longer.

The possibilities for effective floor designs are only limited by your imagination and the degree of effort you wish to put into the project. In the dining room you can stencil a border around the area where the table will be placed. In the bedroom you can pick up a motif from a bedspread and continue it onto the floor. The floor in a child's room can be transformed into a play with stencils of farm animals or a circus train. Use stencils to cover an entire floor surface, or only parts of the surface, leaving a large area of wood. Many subtle effects can be achieved by using stains and varnishes instead of paint. There are a great variety of

Stenciled floor designs can be approached in many different ways. A sparse floral pattern works well on a plain, varnished wood floor (*opposite page*). If you would rather not put a permanent design on the floor, then a stenciled floor cloth may be the answer (*above*).

paints and stains available that are suitable for floor stencils. Be sure, however, to always use oil-based stains and varnishes, because they can withstand the heavy traffic the floor will receive. Japan paint is the best choice for floor stenciling because it is both durable and quick drying. This is especially important because very often you will be kneeling or walking over areas that have just been stenciled when working on a project.

Some wonderful effects can be achieved by bleaching, staining, and painting the floor before applying the stencil.

Courtesy Adele Bishop

PREPARATION

Floor stenciling requires much more preparation than any other type of stenciling. For the best results, a wood floor should be new or completely redone before stenciling on it. Even the best paints will not hold on floors that are ingrained with wax, grease, and dirt. In addition, uneven floorboards, splinters, and indentations will result in an uneven print and will damage your stencils and brushes. On the other hand, some people like the rustic look that can be achieved by stenciling on an uneven or rough floor. If you want to attempt this, be sure to use acetate or Mylar® stencils and have a good supply of brushes on hand before beginning the project.

If you wish to achieve a sharp, well-defined stencil design it is best to have the floors sanded. You can do this yourself with a sanding machine; however, it is a very difficult and time-consuming task. I highly recommend having the floor sanded professionally. Be sure that the sanders do not use too fine a sandpaper when working on the floors. If the surface is too smooth the paint will not adhere to it very well. Once the sanding is complete, vacuum the floor thoroughly, mop it with a mild solution of soap and warm water, and then go over it with a tack cloth once it is completely dry. Dust and grime are the enemies of any stenciling project.

At this point, there are several ways to approach a stenciling job. You can paint the entire floor with a flat oil-based paint to provide a background base color. Use two coats for an even base and make sure the paint is completely dry before you begin stenciling. Oil-based paints take a long time to dry, so I recommend waiting at least two days. You can use latex paint, but it will be less durable and the water in the paint may raise the grain of the wood in places. Lightly sand the painted surface with a fine grain sandpaper in the areas where the grain has raised.

Bleaching is another very effective means for preparing a floor for stenciling. Oak is the best wood for bleaching as it results in a mild cream color. Pine will have a more yellowish tinge. It is best to have the floor bleached professionally.

The process uses very caustic chemicals that can be dangerous if you don't know what you are doing. Once the bleaching is complete, lightly sand the floor to create a slight grain for the paint to grab hold of.

A similar effect can be achieved by a process known as simulated bleaching. This is a way of lightly staining the floor so it appears as if it has been bleached. It is a simple process that you can do yourself. Apply a thin coat of palecream, flat, oil-based paint to the floor and then immediately wipe it off with a rag. You should do small sections of the floor at a time so that the stain doesn't dry before you have a chance to wipe it up. Take care, however, to keep the paint as uniform as possible as you progress.

If a darker, wood-grained effect is desired, take advantage of the many colored stains available on the market. These stains can be used to color a wood floor or to simulate a certain type of wood you don't have. These oil-based stains will quickly absorb into a newly sanded surface and will not adversely affect any paint that is subsequently stenciled onto the floor. Be sure to always test a stain on a small patch of your floor before undertaking the entire job so that you can see exactly how the floor will look when the stain is dry. Wood swatches provided by paint and hardware stores will not give you an accurate picture of what your particular floor will look like. As always, allow the stain to dry for two or three days before you begin stenciling the floor.

While the basic techniques for planning, measuring, and applying the stencils to a floor are the same as with other large stenciling projects, stenciling a floor is probably the most physically exhausting project you can attempt. Be prepared to spend long hours stooped over on your knees applying the paint. In addition, you will be constantly stepping over and around areas you have just stenciled. Wear pads to protect your knees and a pair of white cotton socks (they are less likely to smudge freshly applied stencils). If at all possible, enlist the help of a friend.

PROTECTING THE FLOOR

After you are finished applying the stencil to the floor, it must be sealed if your work is to last. Use a varnish or a polyurethane finish to seal the project. Most varnishes have a polyurethane base of some sort. Polyurethane forms a durable, water-resistant coat that can withstand the heavy traffic received by floors. These varnishes are available in matte, semi-gloss, and gloss finishes. In most cases, depending, of course, on the effect you are trying to achieve, the semi-gloss is the best choice. This finish will make the floor look clean, but not glassy. Also, unless you want the project to have a yellowish tint, buy a high-quality clear varnish. Use a wide, flat brush to apply the sealant and work with the grain of the wood, being careful to avoid brush strokes. Test a small portion of the stenciled area first to make sure that the paint is completely dry and the colors won't bleed. Two coats of varnish will result in a strong, durable floor that will last for years.

A floor stenciled in this manner can be sponge-mopped with a weak solution of soap and water. Avoid abrasive detergents and never use wax or wax-based cleaning products. Any buildup of wax will make future touch-ups difficult. You may eventually have to revarnish the floor if the finish begins to wear off.

If the stenciled floor is in an area that receives a lot of traffic, such as a bathroom or kitchen, you must use a durable polyurethane varnish to protect your design. It may be necessary to reapply this varnish after several years.

FLOORCLOTHS

Another option for decorating the floor of your house or apartment with stencils is to make a stenciled floorcloth. The floorcloth is one of the most charming manifestations of the revival in the art of stenciling. As with other types of stencil decoration, the painted floorcloth was a result of the New England colonists' attempts to beautify their homes using the minimal resources they had at hand.

The floorcloth, a decorated piece of heavy-duty canvas that has been primed with paint on one side then adorned with a stenciled pattern, has been virtually obsolete in both America and Europe since the nineteenth century. In recent years, however, this wonderful decorative piece, along

© Richard S. Mandelkorn

with other forms of eighteenth and nineteenth century interior design techniques, has been enjoying a renaissance. Floorcloths, forerunners of carpets and rugs, were the earliest floor coverings in both European and American homes. They were wide expanses of colorfully painted canvas, decorated with designs that simulated tile floors. Floorcloths served as both an inexpensive means of adorning plain wood floors and as an early means of insulating poorly built homes from drafts. Over the years, artisans began expanding the simple geometric designs of the early cloths into patterns of flowers, trellises, and vine borders.

Today, stencilers are exploring further the immense design possibilities of a floorcloth. Because the floorcloth is a well-defined geometric shape, it is the perfect medium for stenciling techniques. The final effect you achieve will depend largely on the motifs and color combinations you choose. Stenciling a floorcloth enables you to let your imagination and creativity run wild, because you are dealing with inexpensive canvas and not something permanent such as a wood floor.

By alternating squares, diamonds, triangles, and random patterns with striped borders in an array of colors you can

create vibrant effects with simple geometric patterns. Traditional stencil motifs such as birds, flowers, vines, and farm animals work extremely well within the confines of a floorcloth. Quilts offer a fertile source of effective floorcloth motifs. The proportions of a quilt are often very similar to those of a floorcloth, enabling you to copy or accentuate the pattern of a quilted bed covering in a floorcloth for a bedroom or den.

Stenciled floorcloths also enable you to experiment using different application and painting techniques. You can blend the colors within a stencil to create a shaded effect. You can apply the stencil paints with a sponge to achieve a rustic, well-worn look. You can even glaze over the entire surface with a glossy varnish to create a deep, rich, dark color. Floorcloths work especially well on natural wood floors. The wood grain complements the rustic quality of the stenciled cloth.

MAKING A FLOORCLOTH

A floorcloth can be made in any size to fit any room. I recommend using heavy #8 or #10 canvas, similar to the canvas artists use for oil painting. It is available at awning stores, or at sailcloth suppliers and comes in roll widths of 3, 4, 5, 6, and 10 feet (1 to 3 m). If 10 feet (3 m) is not wide enough for you, you can join two pieces of canvas together using a flat seam. Always buy authentic 100 percent cotton duck canvas and transport it in rolls. If it becomes wrinkled iron it with steam. It is important to keep it as flat and crease-free as possible.

PREPARING THE CANVAS

Beautiful stenciled floorcloths can be made with both plain unpainted canvas, or canvas that has been treated with primer. If you choose to paint directly on the canvas the result will be a light neutral background and will, of course, require a lot less work. Priming, however, will enable you to control the background color. A simple off-white background will contrast nicely with dark stenciling

colors such as blue, red, and green. If you choose a dark background color, then you should rely mostly on light colors for your stencil motifs.

If you plan on priming the canvas be sure to allow up to two extra inches (5 cm) in both length and width since this will cause the floorcloth to shrink. Exact measurements, however, are only important in instances where the floorcloth is to be fitted tightly into a particular space. In this case, use a piece of canvas at least six inches (15 cm) wider and longer than the dimensions of the space. This will give you ample room for shrinkage and a hem. You can always trim down the canvas after it has been primed if necessary.

PRIMING AND STENCILING THE CANVAS

Before priming or painting the canvas, clear out a large floor space and vacuum and mop it thoroughly. Dust or dirt will give the canvas a rough uneven surface and you can't sand it down and start over like you can when stenciling a wood floor. Lay down several layers of newspaper to soak up any excess paint that may soak through the canvas.

The best primer for floorcloths is flat, latex paint. Oil-based paint can also be used, but it is much more difficult to work with and takes much longer to dry. You will need two or three coats of primer to prepare the canvas adequately. Apply the first coat lightly, but evenly. This will prime the canvas for the second and third coats, which will provide a good working surface on which to stencil. Allow at least twenty-four hours between each coat for the paint to dry thoroughly. The number of primer coats you apply depends on the texture you are trying to achieve. The more coats of primer you apply, the smoother the floorcloth will be. Make sure to save some of the background paint to cover mistakes. If you make a mistake while stenciling you can always paint over it and start again.

Japan paints are the best for the actual stenciling. They are quick-drying and will last for years. Acrylics are also durable and are a bit easier to work with.

HEMMING AND SEALING THE FLOORCLOTH

The easiest way to hem a painted floorcloth is with a hot-glue gun. Trim the corners to get rid of excess canvas and then turn the edges under and secure them with the hot glue. A good craft glue will also work, but a hot-glue gun is easier to use and the final hem will be more secure. Some of the paint around the edges of the hem may crack during this process. You can touch up the cracks with the extra background paint once the glue has dried.

The final step is to protect the cloth with a varnish. Apply two or three coats of flat or semi-gloss polyurethane varnish depending on what type of finish you desire. Varnish will make the surface water resistant, allowing you to sponge up spills and dirt. You may occasionally need to apply extra coats of varnish to extend the life of the floorcloth. A yellow-tinted varnish can be used to give the floorcloth an antique finish.

Courtesy Adele Bishop

Shelburne Museum, Shelburne, VT

FURNITURE

There is a long tradition of stenciled and hand-painted furniture in every region of the world. In eighteenth-century France, the *gentelise* kept their clothing in large, ornate, gilt-laden armoires. In Provence, chests and commodes were decorated with simple stencils, using a vivid palette that echoed the Provençal countryside. The Scandinavians stenciled flowers and other natural motifs on their furniture, accenting the simple lines with soft, muted colors. In medieval England, churches and the homes of the rich were decorated with elaborately painted and stenciled screens and furniture. The Japanese have a centuries-old tradition of finely lacquered and painted furniture, adorned with patterns that echo the country's detailed wood prints.

Later, in nineteenth-century England, the proponents of the Arts and Crafts Movement turned their attention to the beauty found in design and color of the accessories of everyday life, such as chairs, chests, tables, and other practical adornments. In the workshop of William Morris, poet, artist, craftsman, and utopian socialist, artisans such as Dante Gabriel Rossetti, Edward Burne-Jones, and Morris himself began designing and painting extremely functional, yet aesthetically beautiful furniture of all types. These men and others were instrumental in changing the tastes of their countrymen from a heavy, gilded look to the simplistic charm of hand painted and stenciled oak furniture. Using rich basic colors and formal floral and heraldic patterns, these men not only designed exquisite chairs, chests, tables, and wardrobes, but also silk textiles, wall-hangings, and tapestries.

Another influential personality in the history of stenciled furniture design was Lambert Hitchcock. In the late 1820s, Hitchcock set up a small workshop in Hitchcocksville, Con-

Shelburne Museum, Shelburne, VT

necticut. There he designed and produced a small, elegant, dark-stained or black-painted chair that was adorned with ethereal gilt stenciling. Known as the Hitchcock chair, this delicately decorated piece of furniture remained extremely popular for well over a century. Hitchcock used bronzing powders and sizing compound—an adhesive that holds the grains of pigments—to achieve a shaded effect within the stenciled outlines. Many artisans still imitate the basic designs and methods developed by Hitchcock in his small Connecticut workshop.

As with other forms of country decoration, stenciled and hand-painted furniture was a large part of the American settlers' art. They had an appreciation for painted furniture that derived from their European roots, but developed it into a decorative style that is strictly American. Perhaps the Amish of Pennsylvania made the best use of stenciling and painting techniques in their furniture. In a style that almost betrays their otherwise spartan lifestyle, the Amish used bright, clear colors to embellish the modest lines and practical construction of their furniture. The bright reds, yellows, and greens of their furniture contrasts greatly to the blacks and dark purples of their clothing.

Today, there is a resurgence of interest in glazed, lacquered, stained, marbled, and stenciled furniture. The current fascination with country lifestyle and design has led many people to look at their plain wooden furniture in a different light. A very charming, yet sophisticated effect can be achieved with the addition of a simple outline or motif to a wood chair back or tabletop. Stenciling furniture requires an integration between the form of the stencil and the piece of furniture. The design must complement or enhance the characteristics and lines of the furniture. And, as with stenciled wood floors, the preparation of the wood and the finishing of the project are extremely important for a successfully stenciled furniture design.

A piece of furniture, particularly a small piece, is often a good first project for a beginning stenciler. The entire project—preparation, stenciling, and finishing—can be completed in a small work area, creating a minimum of mess. In addition, stenciling furniture entails working with

Courtesy Stencil-Ease

Courtesy Adele Bishop

a number of small, confined surfaces, somewhat limiting your design choices, but providing enough freedom to be challenging and to help you develop your skills. The best items of furniture to stencil are inexpensive pieces; either those bought cheaply at a secondhand store or new unfinished wood furniture. Never stencil on a genuine antique or a valuable piece of furniture because refinishing will detract from its value as well as its beauty. If you are a beginner and not very comfortable with your stenciling skills you may end up ruining a valuable piece of furniture. The monetary and aesthetic value of new, unfinished furniture and old, but not precious secondhand furniture, can be greatly enhanced with the addition of a well-designed and executed stencil motif.

Tables, armoires, chests, and dressers all respond well to stenciled designs. The extent of your design will largely depend on the lines and form of the piece of furniture you will be stenciling. Limit your stenciling to a specific surface rather than attempt an intricate overall pattern. Subtle borders and motifs work much better than an intricate gaudy pattern that may overwhelm the shape of the furniture.

Step back and look at the piece you are considering. Take note of the shapes and forms on the surfaces of the item. You may want to make sketches of the various surfaces you are planning to stencil, as is suggested in Chapter Three. Measure the various surfaces and carefully draw them to scale on graph paper. This will help you create a proportionate and integrated design, and will train you to look at each surface both as an individual component and as part of a greater whole. When breaking a piece down surface by surface it is important to keep in mind how the overall

Courtesy Stencil-Ease

© E. Silva/FPG International

design will look. A well-integrated design that conforms with the lines of the various surfaces is extremely important when working on a confined space such as a chair, table, or chest.

There is a symmetry inherent in most pieces of furniture. This symmetry can be used to great advantage when designing your project. You may want to plan your design along the central axis of the piece with the remainder of the pattern falling evenly to either side. Or, you may wish to work against the natural symmetry by placing more of the design on one side or the other. Be careful, though—working against a piece's symmetry can result in an awkward, unbalanced look.

It is also very important to consider any curvature the piece may have. It can be difficult to apply flat stencils to a curved surface, such as a turned leg or a rounded chair back. The stencil outlines you choose must conform to the shape and proportions of the furniture. Select stencils that fit in with and complement these curves so that they enhance the shape of the piece rather than detract from it. As a general rule, use small cutouts that don't have to be severely bent to conform with an extreme curve.

Ideas for motifs and designs can be found anywhere. Page through magazines and furniture catalogs. You may find the perfect element on which to base an entire design. Books on American and European folk art provide great examples of traditional color schemes and decorative effects. As with all stencil projects, printed and woven fabrics are great sources for design ideas. Perhaps the best place to look for ideas is in your own home, especially in the room where you plan to display the finished work. Look at the moldings, draperies, carpeting, and other furniture present. What elements can you pull from them and incorporate in your furniture design?

As stated earlier, the preparation and priming of the wood surface of the piece is just as important to the final result as the stenciling itself. As a general rule, stenciling on furniture is most successful when the surface has been treated with some sort of stain, glaze, paint, or gesso. Stenciling on raw, untreated wood will result in fuzzy, ill-

defined outlines. This may, however, be just the rough rustic look you are striving for. On the other hand, if it is a clear, crisp effect you are after, then it is advisable to take advantage of the many paints, stains, and glazes available on the market.

Before doing any type of staining, painting, or glazing, you must be sure all of the surfaces are properly prepared. This is especially important if you are working with an old, secondhand piece of furniture. Completely strip off any old, damaged paint or varnish. There are a number of finish removers available on the market for this purpose. Many of these are extremely toxic, however, so always follow directions carefully and work with gloves in a well-ventilated area. Next, check the piece for any structural defects or damage. Be sure it is free of woodworm, glue together any loose joints, and fill any cracks or holes in the wood with wood filler tinted to match the color of the wood. Finally, sand the entire piece with a moderate grain sandpaper until it is smooth and then wipe it thoroughly with a tack cloth to remove all dust particles.

Glazing or staining produces a much softer, more translucent effect than paint. This soft effect will give the stencils great depth of color. A painted surface causes the stencils to stand out more; however, the color will not seem as vibrant. Depth of color can be achieved on a painted surface by applying a coat of tinted, semi-gloss varnish after the stenciling is completed.

Traditional stenciled furniture usually has a dark solid background color, such as deep red, black, charcoal gray, dark green, or blue. This adds weight and substance to the finished piece. A light floral motif, applied in gold or bronze paint to this dark background is added for a rich antique effect.

Conversely, a light, ethereal effect can be achieved by treating the bare wood with a light stain and then adding a light colored glaze. This stain and light glaze combination results in a thin base that enhances the wood grain, as well as any joints or routed edges the piece may have. Most glazes on the market are clear. They can be easily tinted, however, by adding a small amount of oil-based paint.

Courtesy Stencil-Ease

Be sure that all base coats of paint, varnish, or glaze are completely dry before you begin stenciling. If you use an extremely glossy or smooth primer, you may have to lightly go over the surface of the piece with very fine sandpaper or steel wool to create a surface that will hold the paint. Always wipe surfaces thoroughly after any sanding.

The basic techniques for positioning, measuring, and applying stencils to furniture is the same as it is for other stenciling projects (see Chapter Two). When attaching your stencil template to the surface to be stenciled, however, be careful not to use any tape that will damage the base coat. Masking tape generally works well without causing damage unless it is left on for a long period of time.

In addition to the traditional paints and colors used in stenciling, you may want to consider incorporating a metallic powder in your stenciled furniture design. Metallic powders create a rich, lavish look. To use metallic powder, apply a coat of clear gloss or satin varnish. Leave this until it is almost dry but still tacky. The tackiness of the varnish will hold the stencil in place. Place the stencil card over the surface. Then apply the metallic powder with a cotton swab or a foam eye-shadow applicator, working outward from the center of the design. Be sure to use a different applicator for each color of metallic powder you use.

Once your stencil, whether metallic powder or paint, is complete, it will be necessary to seal the project so that your design will last for years. Polyurethane varnish is easy to apply, will adequately protect the design, and will help to bring out its colors. As stated earlier, varnish is available in three different sheens. Matte varnish will protect but does not have a shine; a semigloss varnish will give a satiny glow; and gloss varnish will provide a hard, shiny effect. You can also add a small amount of oil-based paint to slightly tint the varnish if desired. Tinted varnishes are also available at art supply stores. The number of coats of varnish you apply depends on the type of varnish used and the amount of wear the furniture will be subjected to. Once properly sealed, the stenciled design should last for years. If some wear or chipping does occur, you may have to touch up the design and revarnish.

FABRICS

The decoration of fabrics with painted and dyed stencils dates back to the early nineteenth century. Canvas floorcloths (see Chapter Five) were the first stenciled textiles to become popular. These were soon followed by stenciled bed hangings and coverings, draperies, pillows, tablecloths and napkins, and even, to a lesser extent, clothing. Many times this decorative stenciling was combined with freehand painting.

Again, economic considerations as much as aesthetics led to the development of decorative stenciling on fabrics. The original stenciled fabrics were imitations of elaborate embroidered bed coverings and woven fabrics. The color choices were primarily basic greens, reds, yellows, and blues. The artisans meticulously sketched and cut out very intricate stencil designs based on the period's popular fabrics. They would attach the stencils to the fabric and use cotton balls soaked in dye to apply the colors. The dyes used were very difficult to work with and tended to run and blur in the printing process. In addition, they would quickly fade if the fabric was washed. Today, textile and acrylic paints have made the use of dyes in stenciling obsolete. Fabric stenciling became so popular in the 1820s and 30s that companies began mass producing preprinted stencils that imitated the popular textile prints of the time.

The popularity of this craft was extremely short-lived, however. Due to rapid advancements in the textile industry printed fabrics became widely available and increasingly inexpensive. Today very few examples of these early stenciled fabrics still exist.

The recent popularity in fabric stenciling can be largely attributed to the development of easy-to-use, water-based textile and acrylic paints. These paints produce beautiful, sharp outlines that are easy to shade, darken, and dupli-

An effective design technique is to repeat a stenciled wall or wallpaper pattern on the fabric surfaces of the room, such as the drapes or curtains.

cate. Because these paints mix with ease it is not difficult to produce the same tone and shading with any number of stenciling impressions. Fabric stenciling is done with relatively thick paints so thinning is not usually required. If you do find it necessary to thin the paint, it can be done with water, unlike japan paints which require turpentine or mineral spirits. In addition, fabric and acrylic paints will last through repeated washings and will withstand substantial wear while remaining soft and pliable, making them ideal for clothing.

There are at least as many fabric surfaces in the typical home as there are hard surfaces. Look around your home. There are draperies, bed covers, hand towels, napkins, furniture covers, sheets, pillow cases, window shades, and more. All of these items offer inexhaustible possibilities for stenciling. Consider adding stenciled designs to T-shirts, children's clothes, plain white clothing, scarves, and handkerchiefs.

The fabric surfaces of a room should be the final step in your interior design project. They act as the unifier that completes a balanced design. If you have a stenciled wall in your bedroom, you can continue the patterns and borders you established there on your curtains, or you can just pick a motif from the wall and reproduce it sparingly on the curtains. The same pattern can then be continued on the bedspread, creating a well-integrated design. Another option is to create an entirely new motif for the fabric surfaces, one that complements or contrasts nicely with the other surfaces of the room.

Pillows and cushions are great objects for stenciled designs. Devise a pattern that creates a careful balance with the size of the pillow. Perhaps a thin hatched border around the pillow's edge with one or two small floral motifs that imitate a needlepoint applique. Again here, the pattern choices you make should be made with the themes and designs of the entire room in mind.

On chair seats and footstools, stencils can be employed in the same way that a piece of embroidery is used to decorate a specific area. Create a stenciled cover that fits the specific proportions of the chair and complements the fur-

© Robert Perron

niture's lines and forms. Floral and geometric designs work well on chair seats, footstools, sofa cushions, and padded outdoor furniture. You can even add new life to an old, beat-up cushioned chair by making your own throw cloth. Plain or colored canvas can be cut to size, stenciled, and then used to cover the worn printed fabric. Patterns can be as simple as single-colored checks, polka dots, or stripes, or as involved as elaborate multicolored floral or scrollwork designs.

Shelburne Museum, Shelburne, VT

Every room in the house has a number of fabric surfaces that could be stenciled. This is an easy and inexpensive way to put a personal touch on your overall design scheme.

Fabric paints today are relatively soft and pliable as well as durable; therefore, they are perfect for creating beautiful stenciled designs on bed linens and pillowcases, as well as on comforters, quilts, and bedspreads. If you use a patchwork quilt or a printed bedspread, you may want to pick up one or two elements from it and incorporate them into a design for your sheets. Some slight stiffness may occur on the painted surface, so be careful not to overdo a stenciled sheet pattern.

If you are adept with a needle and thread, you may wish to create yards of stenciled fabric for use in sewing. An article of clothing, a set of curtains, a bedspread—all of these home-sewn items are made even more personal when sewn with a fabric design you printed yourself. The fabric design, however, should be kept fairly simple so that it will not require difficult measuring and matching when it comes time to cut and sew. Also, if you are stenciling a great deal of fabric, the process will go much more quickly when using a simple repeated motif and only one or two colors.

Stenciling on fabrics is extremely simple; however, the basic techniques do vary a little from other types of stenciling. I briefly touched upon these and provided a number of pointers in Chapter Two. Review those pointers before beginning your fabric stenciling project.

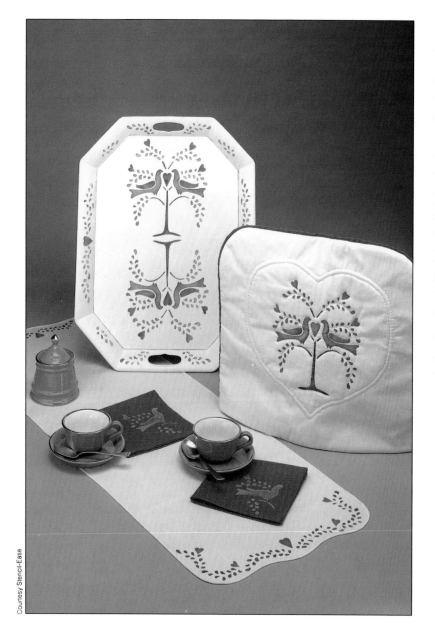

Courtesy Stencil-Ease

CHOOSING A FABRIC

Natural fibers are the best on which to stencil. Their smooth, absorbent surfaces are easy to stencil and create a durable bond with the paint. Fabric that contains some synthetic fibers can be used, but it will not take the paint as well as pure cotton, silk, or linen. The absorbency of even a natural fabric, however, will vary depending upon the weave of the cloth and the peculiarities of the specific paint you choose. So always test out a small piece of the fabric with various paint colors to see if they bleed. Fabrics with a tight, flat weave will also take the paint better. Loose, pliable fabric tends to move and shift during the stenciling process, creating a fuzzy, uneven look. Fabric with a raised weave, a nap, or knitted fabrics do not work well either. The paint rests on the surface of such fabrics and will wear off quickly. In addition, when this type of fabric stretches, the pattern also stretches, revealing the unpainted gaps in the weave.

Any fabric, new or old, should be washed before being stenciled to remove any trace of starch and sizing. You may wish to dye the fabric in the washing machine if you are looking for a specific background color. Once the fabric is dry, iron it thoroughly to remove all creases. Next, stretch it tightly and anchor it over a board or piece of cardboard. This will keep the fabric wrinkle free and prevent it from slipping while you are stenciling it. It is best to anchor the fabric with pushpins or dressmaker's pins; however, masking tape covering each edge of the fabric will also suffice. If you are printing a large piece of fabric, divide it into several working sections and then carefully align the grain and edge within each section and secure it. When stenciling a garment, place several layers of newspaper inside it to prevent the color from bleeding through to the back.

Use the same measuring and marking techniques outlined in Chapter Two. Register marks and guidelines, if needed, can be drawn using a tailor's chalk or a soft pencil. If using a pencil, however, draw lightly to ensure that marks can be easily removed.

© Jessie Walker

Courtesy Adele Bishop

The stencil brushes used for fabrics are the same as with any other project and the paint is applied using the same pouncing motion. For fabrics, it is best to use small amounts of paint at a time. Do not thin the paint at all, but use it directly from the tube or jar. If you use too much paint, or the paint is too thin, it will bleed through the fibers of the cloth. The fabric surface creates friction, making the application of the paint a little more difficult. It is always good to practice on a piece of scrap fabric before beginning.

Keep in mind that mistakes made on fabrics cannot generally be removed. Once the paint is applied, it is there to stay. Keep your work area clean and continually wash your hands to prevent any unwanted smudging. Also, periodically check the backs of your stencils to make sure they are free of paint. If you are creating a multicolored design, make sure the first color is dry before adding the second.

Once you complete the stenciling, allow the paint to dry thoroughly. This usually takes only about fifteen or twenty minutes for most textile paints; however, you may want to wait up to an hour just to be sure. Next, iron each side of the fabric with a dry iron for about ten minutes to set the paint. This heat sealing will bind the paint to the fibers of the fabric.

Stenciled fabrics can be washed in either a washing machine or by hand. The first washing should be done with a mild detergent in warm or cold water. After that you can wash it as you would normal laundry. **Caution:** Some textile paints cannot withstand dry cleaning. Check the label of the paint jar or tube for complete washing instrucions. The final stencil design will be extremely durable; however, some fading may occur with repeated washings or if the fabric is continually exposed to direct sunlight.

Shelburne Museum, Shelburne, VT

THE STENCILS

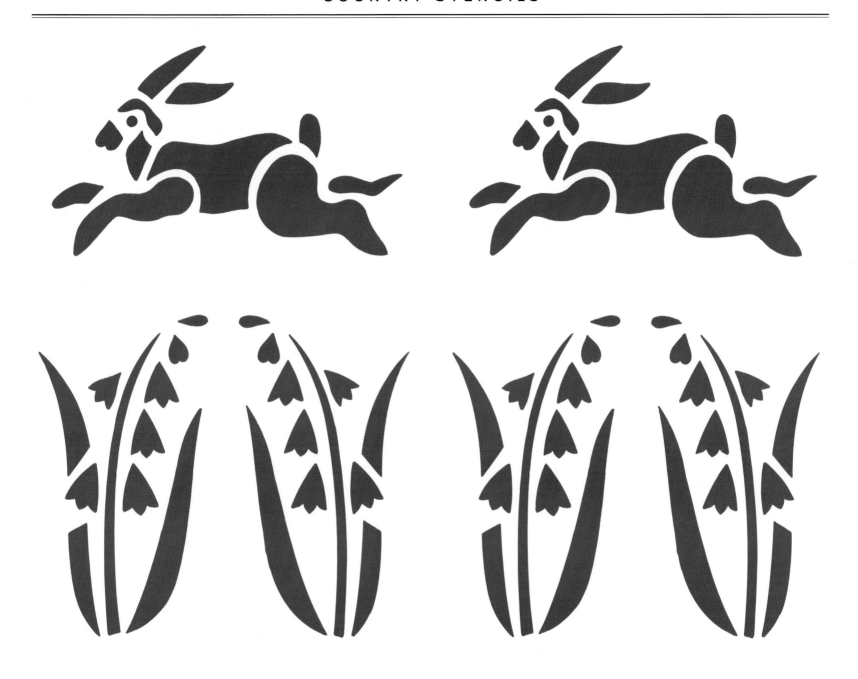

INDEX

Page numbers in italics refer to captions and illustrations.